MADE FROM MY MOTHER'S CEILINGS

JAHMAN HILL

(the first manuscript)

Cover Artist: Harrison DeFalco
harrisonallyndefalco@gmail.com

Release March 2017

Published by:

Printed in the United States of America
ISBN 978-0-9984270-4-1
Published by 310 Brown Street
www.310brownstreet.com
jahill3@crimson.ua.edu

Shards of my mother's

ceilings make me who I am

Fragile, see through, man

For:
Mum and Pops
Gram and Gramps
Kevin, Kim, Momo, EJ, J'Nayia, Jordan, Jayden, Josiah, Ant, Jaleesa, Keisha
Kailey
The BDC
Dr. Boylorn
Nana Neva and Uncle Stan
Dr. Safa
Dr. McKnight
Michael Harriot
Shaun Judah
Escue
Tony
Cheryl
Austin
CPH
and countless Others

Why:
For believing.
For inspiring.
For listening.
For being there.
Thanks.

the Poems

the Foundation, 11
Prayer of Consecration, 13
Mum, 17
Beans, 20
Pops, 23
Brandi's Song, 25
Me, 26
A Poem About Growing Up and Going to School and Pretty Much Life Until Now, 27
Umbrella's Prayer, 30

the Body, 32
Black Body Rhetoric pt. 1, 34
I Grew My Hair Out, 36
Ghost Pepper, 39
the Saiyan, 41
Native Son, 43
Black Body Rhetoric pt. 2, 46
the Moment the Beat Drops Attempt 1 (To Panda and Father I Stretch My Hands pt 1), 48
A Prayer for Black Joy, 50

the Language, 52
the Code Switch (After Steven Willis), 54

Stop Signs, 57
Nice pants revisited, 58
Masculinity Says, 60
Cash Me Ousside, 63
Taye Taye (cuz Eric is beautiful) [speaking is politic], 65
Man Unravels Himself into Pink Mist, 67
Me Trying to Write an Erasure Poem, 69

the Institution, 72
From Younger Me Today (Folding Clothes IV), 74
White Heaven, 76
On the Night Before the Inauguration, 80
Breaking News, 82
donald trump vs. the Black Academic, 83
Gaze, 86
For Mamie Lang, 88
Alternative Facts for Black History Month, 90

the Theory, 94
On Defining Power, 96
Return, 98
Crowded Room, 100
Sometimes, I Wonder, 101
Black Body Rhetoric pt. 3, 103
On the Night the Patriots Come Back and Beat the Falcons and
I'm Reminded What Privilege Is and I'm Pissed, 104
Black Body Rhetoric pt. 4/This is What it Feels Like, 106
How Great (After Chance the Rapper), 109

the Project

For a long time now, I have been wondering what this is, what this project is. It only occurred to me sitting in class today that this is necessary, that *you* are necessary. *We* are necessary in this moment. This project is an attempt to recreate my history through identity. It is an attempt to view my identity through gender. There is a power in that, in the words of this project, a power that is built in its necessity. We are living in a time where the rules have changed and many are asking what's next. A rethinking must occur. This project is me attempting to start that. I believe that poetry can be a powerful tool, a game changer, a prompt of passion. Poetry is honesty, an attempt to change a life. Honesty is not always beautiful, not always clean. Honesty can shatter realities, build new ones, and reinforce old ones. Honesty shifts constantly, from one moment to the next. Honesty will always be there, somewhere, waiting for us to find it. My goal throughout this project is to find honesty within myself, to figure out just who I am, who we are. This is a very socially arduous task. I believe that society is one of the largest factors of the self. Your interactions with others, how you see others, how they see you, influences, almost even determines your identity. Interactions with the world make me who I am, and this project is an attempt to understand both sides of the equation that is my existence. I hope that the result can be called poetry.

My mother is an incredible woman, and there is nothing statistically exceptional about that. She has always been one of my biggest inspirations, and a hero in my eyes. This project is for her, for my dad, for the family. When I say I was made from my mother's ceilings I mean this: my mother has never allowed society to tell her who she could be. Having children at an early age did not stop her from graduating, from getting a college degree. She has shattered every glass ceiling in her path, and I was lucky enough to have a front row seat. I like to think that I inherited her drive, but I'm also aware that I have inherited some shards of the very same ceilings that brought her down. This is a tension that I struggle with everyday, the tension that produced this project, this attempt at honesty, at poetry. Like glass, I am fragile, reflective, sharp. Yet I am learning, I am growing.

For me, race and gender are intertwined. My "gender story" is Black as fuck. It starts with a scrawny Black kid born in Rochester, NY, moving to Kansas. My gender story is spending my younger years on a military base where throughout all the diversity I experienced, I learned to love people who look like me. My gender story is me moving to an all white town in middle school and thinking that exuding masculinity was the only way people would respect my Blackness. My gender story is me going to college and getting "woke". My gender story is me removing all these layers in an attempt to find myself. In that process I found this project, still unwrapping itself, still unfinished.

Understand that this project is a reflection of this moment as much as it is a reflection of myself. I intend to explore what my being here, as a Black man, means to me today, and how we as a society got to this point where I am the human that I am. The goal of this project is not to make you smile and laugh. It is to keep us thinking, preparing, improving.

the Foundation

As for the question of where do *I* begin, the answer lies in the

family, in the faith, in the school. It lies in the foundation. I am a

process of those before me attempting to shape those after me. I

am present, I am the interaction, a bridge between two worlds, past

and future. My foundation is made of lives, legends, and just the

right amount of luck. It is my mom saying yes to my dad and my

dad saying yes to my mom. It is my grandparents being everything

they possibly could for me, encouraging me. It was my family

showing me that sacrifice was something that happened. That I

would have to sacrifice someday. My foundation was love, was

faith, was joy. It was pain, was fight, was loss. Preparation. My

story begins with the making of a boy. The formula was simple:

prayer, love, and freedom. As my family taught me what a Black man could be, I also learned what I thought a Black man should be.

This is my construction.

Born a canvas
Raised a canvas
They gave me a brush
Told me to paint

Prayer of Consecration

and before the Last Supper commences:

All Eyes turn towards the Heavens,

all Heads bowed in preparation for the Prayer of Consecration

by Consecration I mean make Holy

I Mean:
turn some
neckbones into the
Lord's Body and pot
liquor into the
Lord's Blood before
we consume these
collard greens and
Black eyed peas in
the most beautiful
fellowship and
when Grandma
break her foot off in
a Sunday Meal after
Church don't our
finger licking and
smacked Lips turn
into a pair of
Christian crutches?
Don't our full
tummies carry her

13

closer to the Lord?
Do we not follow
along in hopes to
catch some
breadcrumbs at
God's table cuz the
food be so good that
**the Prayer don't
be just a blessing
to the food but be
a blessing to the
hands that made it**

the
Consecration be
that moment
She make us
wash our hands
before we Eat
The moment
that we wash
ourselves into
receiving God's
Word
Turning our
paws into
Cradling Things
ready to place
our hands at the
Preparer's Foot
The Foot they
broke off in the
meal

14

The meal that
we Eat in His
likeness as the
Prayer quickly
becomes

**us folding ourselves
back into a familiar
History**
Rituals I've been able to
recite since I was 5
years old but felt since I
was 2 the Prayer
becoming the moment
we all give ourselves up
in unison all vulnerable
to the way the Spirit
wafts across the room I
swear the smell of
Home Cooking smell
like Jesus Homecoming
the Last Supper turned
into smörgåsbord of
past, present, and
future, forming
redemption how else
can you Eat with friend
and foe alike without
forging some form of
Forgiveness?

How else can

15

He, on the night He was betrayed,
take Bread, give thanks,
and break it,
giving it to His disciples, saying,
Take,
Eat,
for this is my Body, which is given for you;
Do this in remembrance of Me.

How else could on that night,

He takes the Cup;
and after giving thanks,
give it to them, His disciples, saying,
Drink ye all of this;
for this is My Blood of the New Testament,
which is shed for you, and for Many, for the remission of sins;
Do this,
as oft as ye shall drink it,
in remembrance of Me.

And on This Night:

We return to the Consecration.
We return Different.
We return more Holy ourselves.
We take His body,
His blood.

We fellowship.

Mum

On a bright blue chariot I rode through the gates of Hell and graced the sea of fire. The cold steel blue protected me on my journey through Hades as I stood just out of reach of demons' grasp. When my chariot was full of treasure I rose towards the surface only to be met by Lucifer himself, eyes burning with the hatred of countless souls; I was counting on vouchers to escape but the vultures in the air signaled my demise; dem eyes of Lucifer sealed my fate at the gates I could not utter a single word as he grabbed my chariot and sentenced me to a life as the eternal gatekeeper and all I could think was, "Please, don't tell my mom." Lucifer looked puzzled, and with the curiosity of someone with the most annoying full-time job where work is literally Hell, he asked me, "Who?". I told him that I know a woman, who commands the attention of the world with a single glare, a stare that cuts like ice's edge multiplied by Excalibur, she could walk on water if she wasn't so busy raising Hills to move mountains, her children all know her by her first name...Mom. A powerful personality she is as

17

sharp as her glare strong enough to both wear and share the pants in the house bring home the bacon and education she has mastered the art of obtaining masters, she has more than Tiger Woods, except she needs no green jacket just a cap and gown in the kitchen she throws down meals that make her closer to Jesus...I swear she could feed my whole family on 5 loaves and 2 fish, and turn wine into water that flows like tears when she turns our whining into water tears, she has a Black belt in the art of the Black belt, Pooty Tang ain't got nothing on her. She has the willpower of Job which is why she is always on her job, which is full-time overtime and holidays with little pay but guaranteed to pay off she's raised a baby while raising a high school diploma and carried another while carrying a college degree taught classes while teaching her kids class carried the weight of my big head on her shoulders her fire has never smoldered she's always been the brightest flame. If she switched places with Kevin Gates he'd get tired. She is the wings of guardian angels her voice is a direct line to God, her patience is a prayer. A closed mouth don't get fed and a smart mouth will get popped she will knock all your teeth out and make you laugh with a mouth full of gums at the same time. She's my mother, mum for short.

And after I said all of this, Lucifer let me go. He said, "I've heard of her before, and I don't want no problems."

Beans

My grandfather always told me:

Beans are good for your heart
Beans make you fart

And I always thought that this was an interesting
way to love, through gas, that is.
I remember being a kid and going to my
grandparents apartment, the smell of cigarette
smoke lingering
The stove was the site of our satisfaction
The meal:
Hot dogs and pork and beans
You know grandpa and grandma were the meanest
of chefs
They didn't mind breaking off a whole kneecap in the

meal, even if it was a can of beans and a pack of
hot dogs
My grandpa taught me an interesting way to love
It was by being human
By the age of seven I was looking forward to walking
out of the bathroom and my grandma walking in and
commenting on my "manstink"
Just like grandpa, I would warn everyone within
earshot not to go near the bathroom for the next
30-45 minutes
I looked forward to unsuccessfully coating my scent
with Febreze
Boo boo mixed with Lysol
See being human is fun when you embrace it
No one on earth can fart like my grandpa
His stench is unique
I can tell he eats a lot of beans
I can tell he has a good heart
when I hear my grandpa tell me he loves me,

I can hear the sincerity in his song

I can hear him attempting to regain years lost when we would show up and he'd be on the porch lighting up another cigarette

You know my grandpa gave that up for us

His love was always unconditional even if he didn't say it

They say the smell of cigarette smoke never goes away

But my grandpa dropped nicotine like a bad habit and I swear he musta picked up a can of beans right after

Cuz the house don't smell like smoke no mo

It smells like

Love.

Pops

So I am a young Black man and I have had my father who has been around for all of my life and there is nothing statistically exceptional about that, but it is a privilege. When I grow up I want to be just like my dad, except I don't wanna be a preacher, I'm a poet. Still, like my dad, I wanna use my words to save souls and bring people closer to whatever their God may be my dad taught me that my religion is acceptance. It is not judgement. My father taught me that you should not run away from your mistakes, you should embrace them, learn from them, my dad taught me that just because someone else calls your past a mistake does not mean that you have to. My brothers and sisters are not mistakes, they are my brothers and my sisters, my dad taught me that people change. And it is ok for you to change and be proud of it. My father went from a republican to an Obamacan to an Obama man to a democrat. He went from a deadbeat to a dad, from a Patriots fan to a...well we're still working on that part, but my father taught me that anger can be let go. You do not have to hold on to it, you do not have to use it, it does not have to control you. My dad taught me what I believe a good father should be. I remember watching CNN with him after he got home from work, I remember learning that what goes on in the world is important, I remember how after hours of shooting hoops my dad would come outside in his "Big Black Shaq" attire and muscle me around even though every time I touched him he would call foul. I remember watching Monday Night Football with him and my brother just waiting for the commercial so we could try and score a touchdown on him goal line style during the commercial break my dad taught me that love exists in those moments of connection, of family. When I say that I want to be like my dad, I mean I want to show people through my actions that I love so that I don't have to say it, but then say it anyway. I want to spread my message to the sick and shut in and show people I care. I want to be a beacon for those who are lost, I want to inspire the same hope in people that my dad inspired in me. My dad never told me "how to be a man". He taught me how to be. He allowed me to come into my own. And I'm thankful.

Brandi's Song

My melodies stem from the key of your song.
I have grown into a flower from your seed.
From caterpillar to butterfly you have fed me and housed me in
your cocoon
You're the early bird, catching worms that nourished my nested
spirit you taught me to fly
These wings are a product of your touch, more gentle than a
feather
You mastered masonry and paved me a yellow brick road
Instilled in me a lion's courage, straw man's wit, and a tin man's
heart,
Thank you for the red shoes, you've always welcomed me home
When the world tests me I am ready
Your wisdom is the ultimate cheat sheet
And I know I don't listen all the time....well hardly ever
But your advice is like the brain
I only access 10%, but that's all I need to survive
Your mind is the modern day internet...before wifi passwords
As a woman you have broken every glass ceiling and used the
shards to make necklaces so that I never forget the pain it takes to
succeed
I am a product of your incredible
You loved me into who I am.

Me

My name is:

Jahman

Black Activist Intellect

Lover of bacon, basketball, and books

I hate LeBron, Ohio State, and rocks in the bottom of my shoe

Panther, Faces at the Bottom of the Well, and Napoleon

Dynamite shaped me

Furry insects, pineapples, and being stranded in the middle of

the ocean shake me

I like reading, writing, and procrastination with all the fun

adventures it produces

Future foreign policy advisor and poet

You can find me where the free food be at

Hill

Hi, it's nice to meet you.

A Poem About Growing Up and Going to School and Pretty Much Life Until Now

Have you ever walked through winter to build roses out of grass through fingers that extended seasons and knuckles that bruised at the first sign of adversity. Thumbs that were opposable but would bend backwards as if double jointed to join hands with majority. A pinky in need of a savior because it was always afraid of coming up short who always looked to the middle finger overused and battered while busy overcompensating for a ring finger destined to remain alone leaving one finger left so busy pointing towards stifled imagination that he simply handed over his dreams to his third grade teacher and learned to palm a basketball instead. Recess became work and school became break time as the ball pounded the pavement like a body hitting the windshield of a car heading north in search of a brighter tomorrow, traveling so fast that it forgot its roots. Sixth grade was never my specialty. As a new kid I wondered the hallway shell shocked by bombshells bombarding me batting eyelashes with slugging percentages as high as Barry Bonds...My nervousness was the steroid as I stared into the gateways of a privilege they possessed not knowing that as the only Black boy in the school I would be hunted like an antelope who grew up with eagles only to come of age and learn he'd never fly. So I daydreamed wings and soared through class with flying colors. I wonder if they smiled because of my flying colors or because I was flying colored. My crayon box was always used up as I tried to fill in the whites of their eyes with a shade of acceptance. The only colors that worked were pigskin and hardwood, so I became the star athlete and only read books at bedtime. The court became my sanctuary and I threw up prayers that were always answered, I passed scriptures, dribbled holy water on sinners, and laid up offerings til i learned to dunk baptisms in my tattered choir robe. Stained in a sweat that is only earned after performance at the expense of a white crowd. Little did I know I was the modern day Mandingo. Excuse me but this basketball is the only thing keeping me off this minimum wage plantation this 9-5 to support my 5-9 kids ages 1-4 who have hands like boxes, ready to square off with a society that told them they were never good enough to try angles I entered high school as confused as a caveman taking a seventh grade geometry test. I was introduced to a concept of racism that can't be covered in a chapter book. In the space that turns smiles and laughter to smile and slaughter they grinned as they twisted the knife in my back that shattered like a weak backboard I was never taught to bank in my shot at life. They wouldn't give us money unless they knew we'd let it sift through our fingers as easily as glitter shines on a kindergarten project screaming innocence with a delicate freckled face. When our dreams became cemented in sleep I awoke clinging to eyelids that allowed me to live a life built on Nikes and Spalding. Reality tugged at my bedsheets as I entered college ready to pick these cotton fields they call class. At first my surroundings seemed like that of a school, but as slow as the summer comes to a schoolboy my courses became cells, my student I.D. was my identification number and my teacher's masters of appropriation and assimilation they assembled an army of free thinkers who used their brains as weapons and touted untold histories like hand grenades ready to drop bombs on the world. We thought we were being equipped with the unknown, we were actually being prepared for the unspoken.

Umbrella's Prayer

I've never been the one to protect memories with similes I've never hid behind the rain but these lines could work as an umbrella, protecting me from the life drops I want to reign in the rain but its so easy to hide the pain glistening listening manhole covers the whole man inside. when life hits me I counter with faith like Floyd.....may weather bring me sunshine through the moon in the night

So I pray for this umbrella. I pray that you protect me from the fall. When temptations pour like cats and dogs I pray for puppy love and kittens. Forgive me for my trespasses and lapses my life be lopsided, notify me when you open the floodgates of heaven

so that I may dance in the rain to the melodies and

let my movements speak blessings onto others. Let

my step be a stepping stone for those behind me

and my puddles be a reflection of those before. Let

my breath breathe love into the lungs of life, my

smile shine bright for those lost in the dark,

illuminating the struggles of a forgotten people my

craft, craft a path towards a better tomorrow

for those oppressed today, let my past be the

classroom of the present, allow me to recognize your

lesson plan and comprehend the teachings of

yesterday, let my fear only strengthen my faith,

may my faith be the wind beneath my umbrella sails,

I pray for 1,000 flights

the Body

The Black male body is a contradiction. It is power and vulnerability. Strength and weakness. Both superhuman and less than. Necessary and disposable. In this process of becoming, I am constantly learning what is expected of my body, the disruption that it causes. I embrace the protest of my being in space. I struggle with the paradox. The trick about performing Black masculinity is making your body look more like a beast, less like a human. It's almost as if we try to replace "masculinity" with animal. It does not have to be this way. We can reclaim our bodies. The body is power. It is a force. The body is the physical manifestation of miracle. It can be changed as a means to an end. The body is politic. Every movement is a purpose, every breath is a drive. I am still learning that the Black male body can exist outside of violence. This is the process.

Bullets like Black men
So much cuz once you go Black,
You never go back

Black Body Rhetoric pt. 1

There is something about this Black body that makes the red and blue
wrap knuckles white around a weapon,
This melanin melody plays method man to the tune of police baton
percussion,
You're all I need to get by,
By now the lights have winded into quiet hornet's nest hands now up the
window rolled down door unlocked,
The furthest thing from safety,
The law made to make me slave now shines a light on the interior of my
American vehicle,
The Dream-protector wears his badge proud,
Wears his skin like a badge,
Where's his badge?
He stands white between red and blue lights,
There is nothing more American,
He protects the Dream,
I am not
the Dream.
There is something about this Black body that makes me more
nightmare.
Makes me the darkness that lets the Dream shine brighter,
There is something about this Black body that screams from six feet
below,
Says I was manufactured for more than a funeral,
Or unsuspecting tombstones,
There is something about this Black body that survives this encounter,
That remembers it is not the officer that pulled the trigger
That remembers the officer is the gun
That America pulled the trigger

That fear pulled the trigger
Made my body into a suburban home that can sleep easier at night,
Knowing their tax dollars were well spent,
That the blood isn't on their hands
Pontius Pilate turns Conscious Quiet
Resting easy, in peace

I Grew My Hair Out

For those who are wondering:

I grew my hair out to be a beast

I grew my hair out to be a Black man

I grew my hair out because those are the same thing

I grew my hair out to make people afraid

                                   uncomfortable

                     scared

I grew my hair out so white folks would quit smiling at me like I was their friend or something--stop asking me questions about Black people

I grew my hair out so I could smile at white folks like I was their friend or something--please, ask me a question about Black people, ask me a question about my hair, ask to touch it...I dare you

I grew my hair out to confuse white folks when I said big words with an Ebonics dialect

I grew my hair out cuz J Cole and Kendrick made it look cool, I admit it

I grew my hair out cuz I save $15 a week on haircuts, and as a

36

Black man trying to obtain two master's degrees at once, a negro ain't got time

I grew my hair out so people would take me more seriously at the protest, at the meeting after the protest, in the street after the meeting

I grew my hair out to conjure an illusion of power that I really don't have

I grew my hair out and watched people treat me more athlete than academic

I grew my hair out and watched my wallet begin to look more and more like a gun

I grew my hair out into a weapon

I grew my hair out cuz it looked cool

I grew my hair out for nobody but myself

I grew my hair out to prove a nigga named Jahman with nigga hair could still make it in this world

I grew my hair out so that I could watch the looks on white folks faces when I performed better than them outside of a basketball court

I grew my hair out cuz that look they have on they faces makes me smile and feel good and it is not for them so once again

I grew my hair out for nobody but myself

I grew my hair out because I know I have a receding hairline
and all this hair hides it
I grew my hair out because I don't know if it will ever grow back
again
I grew my hair out to fit the description of a Black man
And I grew my hair out to make that the description of a good
man

Ghost Pepper

When my high school English teacher gave me ghost pepper hot sauce,
I was ready to prove my toughness
My manhood
I ignored his warnings
Ignored the kids running out of the room mouths literally aflame
The beef chalupas I had for lunch
And all common sense
I grabbed the bottle and got ready for the Cum shot of my life
But then Mr Scheideman yelled at me
Told me only to do two drops
But I said fuck you Mr. Scheideman
I saw you do 6 drops during homeroom
I'm just as macho as you
And on the 7th drop
My throat became a land mine
And the shrapnel had to exit somewhere
My ass opened...with conviction
Hell fire poured out of my rectal cavern
Heat pulsed from the epicenter of the blast
Sweat poured from my raised brow
As I questioned my own existence

I heard this was called a hot flash
As remnants of the devil's semen seeped into my anus
I literally could not wipe fast enough
My life flashed before my eyes
I guess this was what I got for trying to be cool
It
Wasn't
Cool
At all
When I emerged from the bathroom
A new man
My butthole feeling like your mouth does after using really minty
toothpaste
Mr. Scheideman laughed
I didn't get it
I couldn't understand
How white people could just absorb other cultures
And shit them out
But not feel the pain.

the Saiyan

Hands down
The greatest anime of all time
Is Dragon Ball Z
65% filler episodes
30% dialogue between fighting
and 5% fighting
Nothing captures the souls of 90s babies everywhere
More than when Goku summoned a kamehameha wave
Went kai-o-ken
Or put his hands up
To summon a spirit bomb
I mean what was there not to love about the Saiyans
A race of warriors that Frieza sought to destroy
Frieza, who we didn't know was a man until seasons later
Frieza, the almighty being who had fashioned himself into a
God
When in fact he was no match for a Saiyan
Could not handle the apes masquerading in white face
The full moon turning them back into their purest form
Savage beasts that no one could handle
Every time a Saiyan died
They came back stronger
And Goku died
Every season

Vegeta was the original Harambe

Confused and misunderstood

No matter what he did

Always seen as angry I mean the man had two emotions: pissed and pissed off

But what I didn't understand

Was the super saiyan

Or maybe I did

See the opposite of the ape

Was the ultimate power

The perfect form

I watched Goku go through phases of utter constipation

A practice that led me to shit in my bathtub once

But Goku

Goku did something far worse

His hair went from a kinky Black to a straight blonde

His brown eyes turned blue

Lightning sparked across his body

A field of privilege

As his power level increased

So did his chances of success

When Goku became a killing machine

He dropped everything Black about him

The power of violence

Was now truly his to own

Native Son

Haiku:
Black hands go up and
Bullets fly at the target
Call it a Raindance

Call it the ritual of the native son
Call it me putting my hands down
Only to pick up arms
Call these bullets assimilation
Nahh better yet call these bullets melodies from heaven
I put my hands up in praise as I ask them to rain down on me
In fact call this murder scene a church
Call this hands up a praise dance or a Raindance
But we already called it a Raindance
So let's just call it murder
A mistake
An accident that can happen to anybody
As if prisons aren't prejudiced
Let's call prisons unprejudiced
Let's call trials allergic to Black people
Which is why we won't get one
Let's call George Zimmerman alive
Trayvon dead
Dylann Roof alive
Cynthia Marie Graham Hurd
Susie Jackson
Ethel Lee Lance
Depayne Middleton-Doctor
Clementa C Pinckney

Tywanza Sanders
Daniel Simmons
Sharonda Coleman-Singleton
Myra Thompson dead
Let's call the Bundy Brothers alive
Philando Castile dead
Let's call this a coincidence
Call it not racially motivated
Let's just not bring race into this
Or statistics
Or history
Or facts
Let's just call it the pot calling the kettle...
A kettle
The kettle calling itself a vessel, usually made of metal and with a handle, used for boiling liquids or cooking foods..but not a kettle
The pot insisting that the kettle is a kettle and that a kettle is also a small area in which demonstrators or protesters are confined by police seeking to maintain order during a demonstration
Meaning the kettle is also Black
Or let's just call this scene a kettle
The kettle
A site for the Raindance
The Raindance
The native ritual
The ritual
The act of putting the hands up in request for bullets to make the body holy again
The body
The native son
The native son
Let's call him

Alive

Not dead

Not dying today

Call him

Ready

Black Body Rhetoric pt. 2

22 ways to make a broken Black Body sound Beautiful:

1. The finest mahogany casket polished with a stunning veneer, lined with white satin cloth on the inside, there are two Black arms, the only part of the body not scorched with American made artillery. She was hugging her little brother to protect him the way the arms are hugging the urn her body disintegrated into the casket remains, closed

2. 137 holes in a windshield, each a starting point, the destination: a melanin mirage of weaponry opening to an oasis of bullets with a four year kickback where justice turns a man hunter into a job hunter after they turn body into bag

3. A Dream deterred

4. A Dream deferred

5. A Dream referred to as the low at which one is not, the valley at which one can gaze at from above, the canyon that implies superiority

6. A college diploma mistaken for a GED

7. A GED mistaken for a "get into jail free" card

8. A criminal record mistaken for a forfeit of the right to vote

9. Voting mistaken for true representation

10. This Black body placed in chains-excuse me-cuffs on the side of the street, ready made for slavery-excuse me-free labor

11. Potential viewed through a stained glass window

12. Rant of representative turned advocacy of ally

13. Struggle turned blockbuster

14. Struggling through blocks busted

15. Hands made to look like weapons through aviator eyes

16. The meat on which the Dream feasts, the badge a hunting license, the flag waving open season

17. A species in danger, but not an endangered species

18. Social constructs constructing social barriers

19. The last breath

20. You were never meant to breathe

21. Chalk outline written in a cataclysmic burrough, the catastrophe turned spectacle, the obliteration turned routine

22. Silence

the Moment the Beat Drops Attempt 1 (To Panda and Father I Stretch My Hands pt 1)

It's 6 am in the morning and I don't need no coffee when my song come on. Don't gimme a shot of espresso, just watch the beat drop and my body wake up, take ownership back over itself, become a beast you can't contain, you can't name, check this meme wisdom: if they can't understand your lyrics, they can't call them trash, when the beat drops, my body becomes a land mine watch how pretty my ribs explode, you don't understand when the beat takes control my body takes me back, the beat drop is the most excellent moment in music, the beat drop is a protest, it is an interruption of white noise with Black soul, it makes your body defy the law, watch a beat drop and your spirit scream defiance at the top of its lungs, watch the bass blast yo back out and let that booty bop a beat drop got me breaking out break moves I ain't never seen before, I don't care what nobody say, ain't no 808's in yo

Starbucks, 2 shots of Desiigner and I'm ready to go cuz when that beat drop, my body takes control ain't no police to police this pride slide to left then change to cha cha and can't n'an nigga nae nae like me, when the beat drops my milly rocks, my pops locks, and my grandparents call it electric, the beat be dropping to a chorus of stay woke, the beat dropping is a reminder that I am still alive, that niggas creeping, it means we gon be aight, it means you don't want no problem with me, the beat drops like Black bodies that keep finding thier way back up, the beat drop is the universal sign that we can't stop til we free, when the beat drops

I can be me

A Prayer for Black Joy

I rose up out of bed today with hope
My blood turned to zero gravity
As my lungs expanded
Absorbing all the mysticism of life and pushing out all the
uncertainty of myself
An offering
Intended for the world to reduce, reuse, and recycle into
something positive
A process
I heard was called breathing
This breath
Like my life
Is simply a gift from someone or something I have yet to
understand
It does not mean this body is not meant for this space that it
is in
It means this body is a much needed disruption
An interruption of the mundane
With life
And when I say life
I mean this expression of community
This integral part of us that despite what some may think
Is essential to this machine we call society
I am a butterfly
And every beat of my eyelash is an exponential curve of
potential
The waking moment is the opportunity to change the world

This mouth
Functions as more than a talking point
It is beauty being pushed through a creative space
This Black
Is no mere defiance
It is affirmation
This beating of the heart is not just for protest but for
celebration
This existence is an instance of miracles of tears, prayer and
joy
So this prayer
This prayer is a thank you
An exploration of the happiness of spirit
For this spirit
Exists outside of this plane
Outside the hate
the love
the joy
the joy
the joy
This joy
Has nothing to do with us
So when we capture it
The best thing we can do
is let it free
Share it
Give it
BE it
live.

the Language

Words are almost as powerful as the ears who hear them. Or, better

yet, our language is almost as powerful as the one who interprets it.

My language has always been a harsh attempt to shape reality. I've

always tried to use words to shape my reality the same way society

has tried to use its language to shape me. It is often a taxing

process. Growing up, I always thought the black man to be loud,

uncompromising, aggressive. It reflected in my language. I loved

to curse, I loved to put people down, I loved to use words to

manipulate. I wanted to convince myself that I could use my words

to overpower and control those around me. I missed the point. I am

just now beginning to understand that audience matters. That the

interpretation of your message is the reality that arises, that the

way you listen to others in turn shapes you. Language starts with learning to listen. To what's said and what is not said. This is

where I find my own language.

There is power in
the Word, fight in the Song, but
the ears hold the Truth.

the Code Switch (After Steven Willis)

While one can learn Ebonics
The application can be a little bit tricky
The use of Ebonics cannot be learned by a search through Urban Dictionary
But that is why you are here
You came, for the code switch
Ebonics 205
Contrary to popular belief, the art of the code switch is not something that can easily be taught, for it is a lived experience.
The code switch is not even something that can easily be explained or defined.
See, "code switch" itself is slang for domestication
Code switch is the attempt to transform my Ebony into English
Code switch is the roping of my syllables and consonants into something fashionable for white ears
The code switch is not something that can easily be undone
See before liberals put a name to the term
We just called it acting good for them white folks
Called it hierarchy
We called it sounding proper
Code switching is me tryna serve chicken with no seasoning and a side of mayonnaise
When my momma slapped the taste out my mouth I feared I'd start seeing Black folks different
See the code switch is the trap card in the segregation starter pack
It makes the red eyes Black dragon turn in its brethren to the blue eyes
That white dragon who determines our worth

Our ability to code switch is what puts us into the good graces of close circles
So when I talk white if you close your eyes you can almost see white
Meaning the code switch is me turning my body into a mouth
Into a yes massa
Into an oppressor's tongue
Yet I refuse to parlay proper to prove my palate can produce privilege
Without a way out
See the code switch goes both ways
Means you know when and where to apply language
The code switch allows you to survive in two worlds at once
It's a weapon
A sign that your rules do not follow me all the way home
The code switch back creates community for a chameleon like me
Watch us effortlessly pass through your exams with a vernacular so spectacular my ability to apply Kant to Kanye confuses you
The code switch means that this body is molding itself through language
No
You are not molding me
My speaking ability proves I can operate outside of the system that is your oppression
My code switch brings Kendrick into the classroom
Assata Shakur into the study guide
Speaks Queen Latifah into the lesson plan
My voice means you must account for my presence
And ALL my cousins, too
So when you learn about the code switch
You are not just learning about the survival

You are learning
About the flourish

Stop Signs

I hate people who yield at stop signs.
Like I don't know if they think that *no one is watching*
Or if they think they're cool
Maybe they got somewhere really important to be
But I do too
So maybe *you should stop*
And why they always gotta be in big trucks?
Just because your car expensive don't give you the right of way
And don't y'all try ta tell me that it's better than running a stop sign
You can do that on accident
You don't yield on accident
Yield means I was *told no*, thought about it *and went anyway*
Yield means they spelled it out for me and I *refused to listen*
Don't tell me you *couldn't* see the signs
Don't tell me the open road *beckoned you*
If the sign says stop you stop
Plain and simple

Nice pants revisited

Hi,

You're really beautiful and I wanna walk up and tell you but as I approach your intimidating elegance all I can say is...nice pants. The awkward silence fills the empty regret of not saying anything at all but still I feel as though I could've said something better. I could've told you that you inspire me to be a better man. How you make me wanna turn every negative phrase about women into something positive for you. Change bbw to beautiful Black woman, make hoe an acronym for a woman who puts hearts over everything, for my bitch to mean my baby is touching Cupid's heart. Whore transformed into a universal slogan like Women Have Omnificent and Remarkable Efficacy. I'd reverse misogyny and turn it into what I thought it was when I first heard it: the love of giving massages. Our men would flip prejudice into patience injustice into just listening for once replace inherent social barriers with baby jack terriers or cats if you're a cat person. Slut would mean she loves unconditionally and the T would stand for thanks, thanks for existing and blessing my life with your mere existence. But all I got right now is nice pants, so I won't say anything at all.

MASCULINITY SAYS...

CALM THE FUCK DOWN
AND MAN THE FUCK UP!
DO NOT MISTAKE THE FLUTTER IN YOUR HEART FOR
POWER, BOY
STAND UP STRAIGHT!
WE DON'T DO FEELINGS
SWALLOW THEM TIL YOUR FACE TURNS TO STONE
NIGGA WHAT THE HELL YOU CRYING FOR?
TEARS AIN'T GONNA MAKE YOUR MOMMA WINDOW
UNBREAK ITSELF
THAT'S WHAT YOUR HARD HEAD DO
YOU A MAN
YOU BREAK THINGS
YOU BREAK INTO THINGS
YOU TAKE WHAT YOU WANT
NIGGA STAND UP!
STRAIGHT!
GET THAT SUGAR OUT YOUR TANK, NIGGA
WHAT THE FUCK YOU GOT ON PINK FOR?
THE HELL YOU TAKING A SHOWER ONCE A DAY FOR?

GROW SOME BALLS
LET DEM NUTS HANG
DON'T WASH EM
SWEAT MAKES GIRLS SMILE
MAKE VARSITY
NO PAIN NO GAIN
TELL HER THAT WHEN YOU FORGET THE FOREPLAY
SLICK DICK ASS NIGGA
LYING IN THE LOCKER ROOM ASS NIGGA
ONLY NIGGA I KNOW SMASHED THREE BITCHES BUT STILL
A VIRGIN ASS NIGGA
SPEAK THEIR CONSENT INTO EXISTENCE
SPEAK THEIR NAMES INTO YOUR BEDROOM
DON'T CALL IT RAPE
CALL IT A WHITE LIE
WHEN YOU AND YO HOMIES CALL HER A SLUT
HOLD YOUR TONGUE
SWALLOW IT
LIKE YOUR FEELINGS
LIKE YOU SAY SHE DO
BE A MAN
TAKE UP SPACE

ALL THE SPACE
PUFF YO CHEST OUT LIL NIGGA
HARDEN YOUR HEART TO HIDE THE FACT THAT YOU WERE
MADE FROM YOUR MOTHER'S CEILINGS
THE FACT THAT WE CAN SEE RIGHT THROUGH YOU
THAT YOU ARE FRAGILE
THAT YOU ARE HUMAN
DON'T LET THEM SEE YOU SHATTER
PROVE TO THEM YOU ARE A MAN
THEN PROVE IT TO YOURSELF
SHOW THEM WHAT A BEAST YOU CAN BE

Cash Me Ousside

When the white girl says, "cash me ousside, how bow dah?"
What she means is "catch me outside, how about that?"
She means to say "if you have a problem with me, we can proceed
to exiting this facility under the premise that once we have
proceeded to open air, the rules will not be the same. In fact, it is
highly probable to surmise that beyond these four walls, outside, to
be specific, no rules exist, allowing for us to engage in activities of
which I can best describe as knucking if you are in fact bucking.
After taking all of this into consideration, how might you be
disposed to this proposition?"
When she says "cash me ousside, how bow dah?"
What she means is that she is dropping hard consonants to sound
harder, to sound tougher
What she means is she must create a caricature of Black identity
that is built on negative stereotypes
Meaning her whiteness is reinforcing my Blackness
What she means is her whiteness is just as fragile as my
masculinity
What I mean is I can relate
That I've requested conference in an outdoor location followed by
an inquiry of their thoughts on my proposal in order to prove my
manhood
I too have lashed out in fear of being broken
In fear of being seen as less of a man than them white boys
I know what it is like to be the bully
To mistake violence for a safe space
To turn my body into Tom Brady
My target into Randy Moss
and make a football out of these hands
The funny part is I've only been in two fights
Both of which I lost

In fact, if one were to catch me outside, I would offer that we
reconvene inside at a later date under the supervision of some
authoritative or administrative figure
Basically these hands ain't as powerful as this mouth
And I thought I could build a castle out of dropped hard
consonants and shards from my mother's ceilings projecting the
man that I thought I was supposed to be
So when the white girl says "Cash me ousside, how bow dah?"
I get it
I been there
I understand
We were both reflections of societal shortcomings
Too scared of shattering ourselves

Taye Taye (cuz Eric is beautiful) [speaking is politic]

It is night
and we are all congregated in the kitchen and we are all happy to be alive
and we are all living and the Patriots are beating the Steelers and we are
in the kitchen where the TV is small We are not in the living room where
the TV is big We are in the kitchen and we are close And the size of the
TV shows how important the game is to us
What's important
is that Sister Smith and the Momma Marable broke they whole foot off in a
Saturday meal and they boy came home from the Big Apple and that
apple ain't as sweet as the plate in the microwave right now
And the microwave is old
And it ain't got a fancy plate on the inside that rotate
Cuz some things never change
Old things can still last forever
In the span of time it take for that microwave to turn our food into a
cancered space I tell Eric the Apple Man that Taye Diggs is the finest
chocolate man alive and he says that I haven't even considered Morris
Chestnut and as we argue there
in front of our girlfriends
Who laugh and watch us
The nature of our conversation speaks our being here into revelry We are
beautiful men discussing beautiful men and our identities aren't
compromised

65

I think of what a moment this is

For it has been 10 minutes and my food is barely warm but my heart is now warm and my eyes are now warm and there is a love in the room and even though Tom Brady is winning everything is OK

And nobody can tell me nothing cuz I believe Taye Diggs the finest man on the planet

And I ain't got no mo time to argue

Cuz it is time to eat

Man Unravels Himself into Pink Mist

Man unravels himself into pink mist
Calls it language
Names his power over things
Limits their potential with words
Makes language the art of representation
Recreates images under the border of their words
Calls everything outside the border primitive
Hires border patrol
Builds wall around language
Does not let others in
Calls others Black
Calls other Woman
Calls others magic
But calls them nonetheless
Man names his power over so-called Black things
Makes science the process of naming things
Makes magic the unnamed
The non-man
The less than human
Refuses to put name on white
On male
On race
Racism
On sex
On sexism
But wonders why it keeps us spellbound
Man says there is nothing new under the sun
But claims Shakespeare made new language
Says there is nothing new under the sun

And makes us whitewash our struggle into English
As long as we don't say genocide
As long as we don't call it patriarchy
Says nothing is new under the sun
Implying there is a cycle
Implying there is yet a kingdom for me to come
Implying these words have been said before
As if I am not original
As if white man is not original
Just a repeat offender
A mind that can be defined
Which is to say confined
Which is to say language is explanation of infinity as finitude on repeat

A cycle

U n r a v e l i n g   i t s e l f

Into pink mist

Me Trying to Write an Erasure Poem

An erasure poem is a poem created by erasing words from an existing text in prose or verse and framing the result on the page as a poem. So I started with this idea that I would do an erasure poem of American history. It started with, "In 1492, Columbus sailed the blue" and ended with donald trump having the largest inauguration crowd in the history of America (and you can't cite Obama here because he didn't make it to the final cut of the poem). But then my friend told me that my poem sounded more like a Texas textbook so I disposed of it the same way I see our country dispose of Black bodies. The poem wasn't even three fifths of our history anyway.

Anyway, I decided to do an erasure poem on racism, on race, and I didn't know where to start. Like I didn't know how to separate race from racism. Like I couldn't erase racism without erasing my Blackness, and I didn't wanna do that and the worst part is these funny lines kept popping up in the poem like "I don't see color", and "you're not like the other Black people I know" and for some reason I felt accepted but when I looked in the mirror my skin didn't sound the same. Which is to say my senses were all messed up sense most of us are either color blind or color bound and I am still trying to find the in-between and at the end of the poem I found myself at whiteness. And there was nothing to erase. Whiteness itself was the erasure. Meaning whiteness Is not what is, it is what is not. Whiteness found it's way into my poem by being not Black, by being not Latino, by being not foreign, by being not a problem, by being the purity we were all aspiring to,by being something that could never really be obtained but certainly could be lost.

My white girlfriend is working on erasure poem called dating me. Meaning her kids will look more like targets. Meaning it is the erasure poem that isn't supposed to happen. The one we are not supposed to allow.

My masculinity erasure poem is called middle school. Is called me trying to hide my middle name to be more like a man. Is called me cursing my parents for naming me Ariel, cuz no, I am not *the little mermaid.* My masculinity erasure poem is me removing bitch from my vocabulary and thinking that meant I wasn't a misogynist. Is called me covering up my sexist beliefs with silence. And isn't that what an erasure poem is? You are not really deleting anything you are just silencing a voice that wants to be heard, the funny thing about language is we think that silence is nothingness, but I like to call it white noise. It sounds like the space in between breaths when white kids are saying nigga to sound cool in front of their white friends. It sounds like me calling my friend gay in that middle school locker room, sounds like me driving with the boys on a road trip, with nothing to say at all but the lyrics to the misogynist rap songs blaring through the speakers and stories of girls we tryna get with. It sounds like the his & hers gifts section at the store on Valentine's Day. Silence is the sound of throats being crushed under the oppressor's boot, intentional, or unintentional. So next time you hear the quiet, listen for the remnants of those uner your feet. Just because you don't hear them crying out, doesn't mean they aren't there. It might just be

An erasure.

the Institution

Black masculinity has always found itself in a struggle with "the Man". Growing up, you learn not to trust institutions. No one has to tell you, the institutions themselves tell you where you stand. If you listen close enough, you can hear it in the way America does politics, education, religion. There is a certain "not belonging" that I feel in all of these places. Institutions shape our history, our government, what we call "real". Institutions determine what we view as success. They mold our identity. Society produces institutions that in turn reinforce the status quo. We must attempt to trouble these narratives and resist subjugation. Black masculinity is often portrayed as the evil that women should fear. The beast lurking in the night. We must not accept this. We must recreate ourselves.

The schools, the churches, the government
Call me enemy.
I fight back.

From Younger Me Today (Folding Clothes IV)

"Niggas from the hood is the best actors,
Gotta learn to live in ways that's unnatural"
- J. Cole

Dear Jermaine Cole,
If niggas from the hood is the best actors, what does that make me? Me, the nigga from Kansas tryna act hard in front of all these small town white folks. Every morning that I wake up, I put on more armor, the secret is when I go to bed I never take it off. The weight is so heavy at times it is hard to stand up straight. I am just now starting to remove these layers. It will be years before I'll be able to really feel again. Me trying to prove I'm Black and male to the white folks means knowing every word to their favorite rap songs, to be oddly homophobic, to be the life of every party. My masculinity is a performance that I gotta put on everyday. Cuz I don't decide my Blackness, these white boys do. These white boys who tell me other white boys are Blacker than me cuz they better at basketball, or cuz they say nigga. So, J, I put on for my city, but the only trapping I do is becoming a Black man performing Blackface in fear of being called an oreo. Call my Black masculinity a makeup kit that I spend hours with in front of the mirror every morning. Cuz to not be Black is to be a bitch and to be a bitch is to be a woman and to be a woman is to be a less than, as if they didn't treat me as a less than in the first place. J, them other boys don't have to

try, they just are. They just are. I don't hate my skin, but I hate the man it wants me to be. That they want me to be. That they think is worth something, is real. Why can't I just be Black. Why can't this skin, this body, be proof enough.

Sincerely,
Me

White Heaven

So last week I was informed that when Black people go to heaven

They will go through a purification process

And God will turn them white

Like everyone else in heaven

Real talk

You get a gold halo

White wings

A white robe (that's probably hooded)

And they will finally be returned to a God-like image

The curse of Ham lifted

Now

Before I chalk this up into the craziest thing I've ever heard at a historically white college or university

I got a few questions cuz who knows?

They might be right!

Firstly

Does God turns us white before or after we get into heaven?

Like
When we die,
Does our Black skin fall off of our white bones
Or do we Michael Jackson moonwalk off our
melanin
Strutting into a lighter shade
Do we remove our Black like a coat?
Does God hang it on the nearest tree while we all
watch and take pictures for postcards?
Is the halo actually a finely toothed comb that you
can't fit on your head if your hair nappy
Do they sell Blue Magic and Palmer's Cocoa Butter
at the angel super market
Or just mayonnaise?
Or do we just shed our skin to the sound of
privilege
Seeping into our souls
After waking up morning after morning to streets
paved with gold cuz God apparently just LOVES gold
Do all of these riches we obviously couldn't have
earned in our short lives make the Black skin just
wanna crawl off our bodies
Is that what inheritance feels like

Question 2:

If everybody white, do anybody clap on beat?
3:

Is this what they did to Jesus?
When He died on the cross?
All wooly haired and what not?
When He cried out,
"My God, my God, why have You forsaken Me?"
Did God look back down and say
"You shoulda been white
Don't know why You asked to be colored
Why You asked for all that excellence You know it
come with a cost
Don't get cross with Me Young Man
It woulda been easier if You didn't pick the struggle
I warned You that if You hung out with the
murderers and thieves You would hang with them
too
When You save them they gonna call You white
anyway
They will wash You white as snow
Clean You up for the camera
You know they say good deeds smell like Clorox
bleach
And have the same effects

Watch them do You the same way they do history"
Cuz honestly I don't think God would say that...
Last question:
If God turns me white
What will I think about Black people?
Will I look at them
The same way you look at me?

If so
To hell with that

On the Night Before the Inauguration

The sun don't wanna set tonight
It wants to reach up into infinity and hang on for dear life
Does not want to be the one blamed for what will happen
tomorrow morning
When it rises and brings a new man to that American
throne
The sun don't wanna see great again
It just wants to hang
Out well into the night
Does not want the street lights to come on and for
momma to call it home
Cuz who needs stars anyway when the sun shine so bright
The sun don't want anybody thinking about darkness
When they look up
Unless they looking up to a dark man
Like we have been
For a while now
The sun don't know that tonight is the last night the
tuscaloosa movie theater will play moonlight
Doesn't know people walked out during the first gay love
scene
That the theater grew empty
And the stars shown into nothing
They just shined for nobody
All pence-ive and no action

If the sun would just go down
Just give up
He would realize that tomorrow I will drive an hour to the
movie theater in Hoover
Just to see its absence
The only form of protest I know now
I will cancel my plans to go to the gym
I will hold my girlfriend's hand as the first real love scene
commences under the moonlight
We will watch the forbidden
And we will not leave
We will just thank the sun
For shining
And giving us
Our shadows

Breaking News

Nigeriaaccidentallybombsarefugeecampwhilehunting formilitantsandlifecontinuesiLeavemydeskforameetin gtheNewYorkTimesheadlinereadsBREAKINGNEWSiw onderwhataboutitisbreakingasnooneasksmeifl'vehear daboutitbecauseeveryoneslivescontinueUNINTERRU PTEDandiwonderwhatamIdoingwhyamIdoing

Here.

donald trump vs. the Black Academic

In the case of donald trump vs. The Black
Academic
The verdict reads:

America
Do we really even need a verdict?
I mean I'm standing right here
You think one election could take me down?
Last week
1 donald trump was elected
This week
Over 4.5 million Black people hold at least a
Bachelor's Degree
Do the math
On November 8th
Our country elected another racist, sexist,
xenophobic bigot to the White House
On November 9th
I still had homework to do
My degree wasn't nullified
I still spent hours in Biology
Psychology
Astronomy
Ecology
International Economy
and yes
African American Studies
because

this African American studies
America
You thought Donald would make America great again
Cool
Black been great
If you studied, you'd know that
You'd know that
Nyansapo: the wisdom knot is Adinkra
Means wisdom, ingenuity, intelligence, patience
Means a wise person has the capacity to choose
the best means to attain a goal
Means the degree is only a stepping stone on the
path to excellence
Means I can learn how to use your tools to
dismantle your system
Or make some new tools or new system if I feel
like it
America
Did you really think Donald could keep down this
cap and gown?
Watch a Black woman reach up and disintegrate the
glass ceiling with a diploma
Watch her cap protect her head from the ash
Watch a Black man step out of Black brute
Zip up robe and put on Kente stoll
Each pattern a proverb
Call this Black graduation ceremony
A statement
Call it Black on Black
Don Black cap
Ready to clap back
On any fat cat who say ain't nobody readin'
I'll watch Pooty Tang, Atlanta, and listen to The

Life of Pablo all while completing a dissertation
on the Comparative Strengths of Tensile Metal
Beams Under Natural Distress
Cuz this Black don't crack
Be excellence in its imperfection
Exceeds expectations
Patience
If I could fit all this education into this poem
it would go something like this:

[Boy.]

But I only got three minutes
But that's all it will take to show Mr.
Apprentice
Who really got the Masters
In the case of donald trump vs the Black
Academic:

That ain't even a question

Gaze

Haiku:
Woman silenced for
Quoting Black woman
Legislated sexism

I watch a woman speak of woman
Of Black woman
Of forbidden
I see the Senate floor wake up and shake off it's dust
Reach into it's memory and pull out a rule
The rule says "Woman, don't speak"
But it sounds like "SENATORS IMPUGN THE MOTIVES AND THE
CONDUCT OF OUR COLLEAGUE -- I CALL THE SENATOR TO
ORDER UNDER THE PROVISIONS OF RULE 19."
Rule 19 says "Woman do not speak the truth about man"
Rule 19 says "Your Black woman's words carry no weight here"
Rule 19 is the stop sign at Coretta Scott's intersection
Undoes the 19th amendment
Makes me notice that all the men in the room are being aided by
unnamed women
As they call on their patriarchy to un-name Elizabeth
And the Senate floor is awake now
And it is He
And He is angry
And He is history
And He see His match
So He places His history into the air
As it weighs on the rib cages of everyone in the room
And all breathing becomes labored as everyone remembers their

roles
And it is 1787 and the chambers echoes
And you can hear remnants of muted women screaming into the
night
As our founding fathers say "We the White Men"
But it sounds like "We the People"
And it looks like "We the People"
And it looks at Elizabeth
And it stares and says "Why are you here? Why are you
speaking?"
And I wanna say something
I wanna stop the madness
I wanna keep it from silencing her
Keep it from defeating her
Keep it from forcing her down
But the problem is I am more it than I am Elizabeth
And I am just sitting there
I am just watching
Waiting
Writing.

For Mamie Lang

Between 1877 and 1950, around 4,000 lynchings occurred throughout the South. Most of these lynchings occurred in front of mobs, where whites would gather and watch, like movies. While there are efforts to put historical markers where many of these lynchings occurred, most are met with resistance. It is important we maintain this history, in whatever ways possible.

My sister is 6 years old when she first learns of lynching. As my mom explains the process to her and my three youngest brothers aged 8, 10, and 12, my sister tells me she thinks lynching is really mean. I do not think this is too early for her to know her history; to know of Mamie Lang, who at the age of 7 fled the south with her family.
Mamie, whose father was threatened to be lynched. Mamie a child was forced to grow wings, another crow migrating north for winter, trading in rope for redlining, fleeing from lynchings in Mississippi, then white mobs in Illinois, then the Klan in Ohio;
I wonder when her wings got tired. How long must a bird remain in flight before it realizes it has no home, that the soil is not meant for their feet
My siblings are not even teenagers before they learn that Black people jump so high because they never know when it is safe to come back down again
Resilience is flying
It is sprouting your wings before you even learn to walk
Call this Black skin an albatross I can fly in my sleep
Try having strange fruit as part of your kindergarten curriculum
And see if the Heavens don't seem within reach
Death ain't nothing more than a runway
Racism won't instill fear it will instill flight
My siblings all ready to soar in spite of what anyone may say, do, or think
Mamie Lang Kirkland landed back in Ellisville, Mississippi 100 years after taking flight, 2 years ago.

At the age of 107, she knows what happened to her
father's friend who returned to soon, only to find nesting in
a gum tree, strung up and shot down to the delight of
whites for his interracial relationship,
In 1919, the man's body burned to ashes and in 2015,
Mamie returned home a Phoenix
Her wings covered the entire city as her fire was
inescapable
The town engulfed in her flame did not burn
And no one could tell her nothing
Not a lynch mob in Mississippi, not a white riot in East St
Louis, not a Klan rally in Alliance
Mamie perched herself on the soil where that gum tree
once stood.
Became a living historical marker.
She Remained.
She would leave when she was ready

Alternative Facts for Black History Month

Jesus was white.

Christopher Columbus discovered America.

George Bush actually cared about Black people. He hired two. Even though one was so light skindid that he didn't even know he was Black, it's still two.

#PaperBagTest

More alternative facts:

Miley Cyrus invented twerking.

Elvis created rock & roll.

Eminem? Greatest rapper of all time.

President Obama's election proves we've made progress in race relations. But...

President Obama ruined race relations.

So...

We elected donald trump to improve race relations.

He's orange, not white

#AlternativeShades

Just kidding.

The elections were in November

We weren't thinking about race relations then

It wasn't February

Why are you Blacks always trying to hog a headline

I mean

More alternative facts:

The NFL is nothing like slavery

There are white players on the field too
They usually call the plays and throw the ball
They are basically a coach on the field
And we love their field vision
But make no mistake:
We have Black overseers--I mean quarterbacks too!
#Diversity
More facts:
ISIS is to Islam as the Klan is to Christianity
The only difference is capitalism
Capitalism creates amnesia
I mean
America treats slavery like its it's deadbeat grandfather who died years
ago when America is the one with Alzheimer's
Now let's have a moment of silence as we remember those killed in the
Bowling Green Massacre

Wait....

Were there any.....

My bad #HonestMistakes
Here's a good one
The civil war was about economics
I mean state's rights
I mean law and order
I mean pancakes
The civil war was about pancakes.

Are you distracted?

Are you not thinking about slavery any more? Good!

More alternative facts:

Sandra Bland killed herself.

Philando was asking for it.

Mike Brown was asking for it.

Rekia was asking for it.

Have you forgotten what Black skin is?

Do you remember the people you immortalize?

Look at your history month

Who do you celebrate?

Did we kill them too?

Do you tell your children what we do to your heroes?

Do you tell them why we gave you February?

Because the month gets snuffed out too soon

Earlier than expected

Don't the 28th feel like Tamir?

Like Trayvon?

Do you tell them what we do to those who speak out?

Do you even know why we say all lives matter?

Because all lives matter is an alternative fact.

What we really mean is you can live a little bit longer if you can jump high enough

We'll give you 29 days and call it a leap year

#Athleticism

Fun fact:

If you're 6'2" or above and white

It's more likely you'll be a CEO or President

If you're 6'2" or above and Black
It's more likely you'll be on the basketball team or seen as target
If you're 6'2" or above and a woman
The world will call you ugly
And it's likely you'll get nothing
#TallPrivilege
More alternative facts:
A poem won't change a thing
Three minutes is not enough time
Why are you still writing
Why are you still believing your activism matters
You are just a Black life
A face made for February fodder
Why can't you just listen
Stop fighting
March is coming
We will end you
Twenty-six
Twenty-seven
Twenty--

the Theory

Reading changes you. It is the process of opening yourself up to

yourself through another's words. Books(music, poetry, etc.)

function as brain food. They introduce you to new ideas that you

come to understand through your own experience. I have learned

so much about myself in the waning hours of the night on the toilet

with a book in hand, emitting waste from one end while absorbing

knowledge through the other. My self awareness has increased

exponentially since starting grad school a few short months ago. I

feel like a completely different person than who I was last summer.

The primary reason: reading. My ideas of gender, race, and the self

have been shaped by countless theorists, authors, poets, academics,

artists. They have helped shape me into the man I am today, the poet I aspire to be. They helped me explore life in a whole new

light. I decided to write about it.

And at some point
We find ourselves trapped in our own minds.
And so we read.

ON DEFINING POWER

THE ROOM GROWS TO SILENCE
AS THE MAN OF THE HOUR STEPS UP TO THE MIC
OR THE PHONE
OR THE KEYBOARD
HE HAS BEEN GIFTED WITH THE ABILITY TO SHAPE HISTORY IN
140 CHARACTERS OR LESS
TO DICTATE FOREIGN POLICY BEFORE HE EVEN STEPS INTO
OFFICE
TO RECREATE THE WAY WE DO POLITICS
OR MEDIA
OR LEGITIMACY
I WATCH THE MAN OF WORDS, WHO HAD YET TO DO
ANYTHING AS PRESIDENT, JUST SAY HE WILL DO THINGS AS
PRESIDENT, BECAUSE HE WASN'T YET PRESIDENT
CALL A CIVIL RIGHTS LEADER A MAN OF TALK AND NO
ACTION
WATCH AS THE KEEBLER CHEESE AND CHEDDAR CRACKER
PISSES ON A LEGACY
WATCH HIM EVISCERATE PROGRESS
AS IF HIS PRESENCE
HIS POSITION
IS PROOF WE HAVEN'T PROGRESSED AT ALL
AND THAT IS WHAT I AM AFRAID OF
THAT ON THE DAY WE CELEBRATE THE BIRTH OF A DREAM

WE AWAIT THE INAUGURATION OF A POTENTIAL NIGHTMARE
AND THIS IS POWER DEFINED

Return.

The worst part of growing my hair out is that I never go to the barber shop
But I went today
I walked in and watched jazz stir itself into a melody
Build a heartbeat outta this jagged hairline
And take me back to trips to the barbershop back in 03
When the third chair was always occupied by it's barber who I never saw cut a single head
But would always say "Tennessee Titans man" when I walked into the shop
And 14 years later and 4 states south
My mouth became a sight for community
Happy as the barber shop
The head nod erasing the time between our last meetings and breathing familiarity into our presence
This performance of connection
And Terry says
"Give us some spoken word
Turn your voice and this jazz into the most redeeming communion"
But I wasn't ready for forgiveness
I wasn't ready to give myself back to the barbershop
But they were ready to give themselves back to me
I came for a edge up and they were ready to shape up my soul
And words of my truth poured out my mouth
And I became a vessel of histories explaining themselves into the now
And the barbershop reminded me that my words are not alarm clock
That they have one eye open
But I notice the one eye closed

As Bently has me read his honesty in the form of rhyme to a
room full of hope
And the room becomes relief as the tension rises to the tune of
heated exchanges
And signifyin
And love
In the most masculine form as we all open our hearts
If for only a moment
And we laugh
At our vulnerabilities
And the room becomes a shared space of feeling
As I freestyle my way into acceptance
And we laugh our way into each other
And Bently tells us about his grandma
And her story commands the room
For this moment
And the shop opens its other eye
As the first chair says
"I don't wanna hear that love poem shit
Give me something with purpose
Something I can learn from
Something that turns my heartbeat into an opportunity for
change
Cuz lately, I haven't seen any"
And he sees me
And I try to turn my words into a blessing
And I speak
And I love
This business built on relationship
This building reaching for something greater
Reaching.
For something.

Crowded Room

Four people stand in a crowded room.
Each person a match
The room is made of gasoline
Crowded by non matched individuals
Pyromaniacs
Wanting to spark up a conversation
Watch the room burn down
Skin made from fireproof
Maniacal smiles a heat wave
But
Four people stand in a crowded room.
Each person a match
They do not match the others
Their skin seems more agitation
Fit for formaldehyde
Fit for a strike
Or a sit in
Or a march
Cremation is the process of turning death into something indiscernible
An attempt to cheat history of its own story
To let nature miss out on having to clean up its own mess
To literally erase evidence from the Earth
But
Four people stand in a crowded room
Each person a match
Afraid to strike anything
Because they fit the bill
Fit the description
Are the prime example
Of a reason
To fire

Sometimes, I Wonder

Sometimes I think Young Thug donning a dress is appropriation.
Sometimes I think the Black man is the white man of the Black
community.
I wonder, how can you both wear women's jeans but still refer to
women as bitches
I wonder if I'm mixing up gender bending with respect
Sometimes I watch Young Thug's music on YouTube
I wonder what makes him so deserving of women's clothes, but not
the women in his videos
Young Thug may not see gender, but he still views women as objects
I wonder if Young Thug considers himself color blind
I'm all for breaking down gender norms but how bout we break down
this misogyny
Sometimes I listen to Young Thug
Sometimes I sing along to his songs
Sometimes I dance
I wonder what this makes me
I wonder if I screamed out not all Young Thug supporters are sexist,
would people believe me?
I wonder if acknowledging Young Thug's misogyny is enough to
vindicate mine
I wonder if knowing all the feminist theories will make me look like
less of a perpetrator
I wonder if I repeated that I'm not sexist enough times I wouldn't see
how I reinforce sexism everyday
I wonder if I schooled people on the differences between sexism and
misogyny, if they would think I was neither
I wonder if I'd be accepted

I wonder if I'd be loved
But sometimes I gotta remind myself that it's not about me
Sometimes I gotta remember it is about the fight
Sometimes I gotta swallow my own pride and admit I am in a system
that benefits my Black masculine body by putting Black women down
But sometimes I wonder
And sometimes I'm wrong

Black Body Rhetoric pt. 3

Sometimes we tend to forget where we came from
As if every Black body was made with a penis
As if bullets were the only holes in the body
As if a woman's story was too bland for the YouTube viral
Sometimes we tend to forget where we came from
By we I mean I
Saw the forgotten woman who raised me put resolve into her jaw
Clinched it as my hair grew and I turned more into a target
More into her likeness
Her living contradiction
My sister's living contradiction
Made to symbolize the start of life and most quiet death
They don't march when the blood turns cold
Google returns no results
"Did you mean *his* body?"
Did you mean to escape the phallocentric
Maybe the death of a woman at the hands of a man is so common they
call it patriarchy
Make it sound more academic and less coffin closed
Maybe equality is the way her name is whispered so softly that she fades
into an invisible tombstone
Placed on an invisible ceiling
Made to feel like glass so you can still see the Dream
Watch it fade
Made to silence what we like to call
Feminism

On the Night the Patriots Come Back and Beat the Falcons and I'm Reminded What Privilege Is and I'm Pissed

There is something about the way a chair flips in anger
The way it sprouts wings and flies
Clumsily
For the first time
The way it falls and the rage subsides
I think the chair isn't as funny as the anger
And the things the anger makes me do
The way it makes me view an object as something to put my power onto
To show I have control
With every Tom Brady first down throw my fists turn into clobbering things
I'm lucky chairs don't bruise easily
They just absorb the blows
They just sit there waiting for me to have done my business and walked away I wonder where we would be without chairs to hold us up
When the announcer refers to Matt Ryan's two shades too dark receiving core as "weapons at his disposal" I feel my skin crawl
My skin knows it's a weapon
But how high must I climb for it not to be
I feel like a dirty bird
And the chair is just sitting there staring at me

And I feel like Clint Eastwood but the chair is still sitting there staring at me
Mocking my frustration
No matter how hard I hit it
The chair is still a chair
And I am still inadequate
My hands are not enough
I don't know how to explain the Patriots to people
The way they dawn red white and blue
The way they walk around like they own the place
And they do
And I am nothing more than a dirty bird
And the chair is just staring at me in defiance
Daring me to get up
And the room begins to fall out from underneath me
As the chair plummets back towards the earth
Waiting for me to move
And I am still a dirty bird
And the dirt is not coming off
Yet still I rise

Black Body Rhetoric pt. 4/This is What it Feels Like

They be afraid of us
Afraid of all this Black
In all this body
Cuz when all this melanin meet all this education we surpass
generalizations
They be scared
They scary
Of all this Black
In all this body
The way we made it this far and we ain't behind bars
Yeah
They shakin in they boots
Cuz Black vernacular so damn spectacular
They couldn't capture it all
Ain't no way to put it in a book
Or whitewash my beaten body slang
This kinda language can only come from survivin that airtight box
they try to put us in
They be gettin ghost
The way we catch that spirit
Make our bodies into something they can't predict
Become one with OUR God
A feeling they can't trigger
A praise they can't beat into submission
Yeah
I'd be scared too
If I snatched the crown off a Queen and gave her lemons for her
gold cuz

Well
When you gave her lemons she made lemonade
Yeah I wouldn't wanna be Becky
My hair got more pride
More defiance
Always defying the laws of gravity
The way this Black skin defies the Dream every night
We live despite your blatant, subliminal, subconscious, and your
id
Racism, liberal racism, assimilation, gentrification, straight up
annihilation, genocide, pesticides, George W. Bush, Antoine
Dodson, Raven-Symoné, trump, Ben Carson, Steve Harvey's
mustache, chitlins, Stand Your Ground, If They Gunned Me Down,
Hand Up Don't Shoot, grand juries and they failed indictments,
LeBron James and his failed hairline, protests that you call riots,
protestors you call thugs, All Lives Matter, the red squigglies all
throughout this typed poem, and BET
We still here
In all our Black Excellence
Fin ta make a way outta no way
And we know you watchin
Wantin to be us
Wantin to be Black
And loud
And proud
And alive

        and

        This is what it feels like
        To be Black
        And educated
        And elevated
This is what it feels like to be the future of a generation
        You. Me. Us. We.

We be the engine, the wheel, the tires but never tired
We lift every voice and sing
Til earth and heaven ring
Ring with the harmonies
of future Barack's and B.I.G's
Michelle's and Taraji P's
They tried to close the doors but we got major keys
These notices of education
But notice that this is not the end
There is so much more for us to build
Refer to your diploma as the foundation to a better future
This cap and gown your training gear
This ceremony a rites of passage
We made it to the frontlines
And they fin ta feel all this Black excellence
From accounting to theater, math to dance
We do this
Cuz we the future
We the wise
We the ready

How Great (After Chance the Rapper)

How great is our God

Sing with me

How great is our God

And all will see

How great, how great

Is our God

So I'm watching the Grammys

And out of the darkness I see a light brown boy in

a funny blue sweater

Like blue ain't my favorite color

Like I don't love ugly sweaters

And the brown boy got a blue hat on wit a 3 on it

As if 3 ain't my favorite number

And he starts rapping

And he's got bars

And he's got soul

And he's got God

He looks directly into my childhood and speaks it onto the Grammy stage

As the lights come on hip hop collides with church and I am suddenly thrown back into 2001 and St. James CME is bumping

And it is 2009 and Escue Chapel CME is bumping

And it is 2017 and St. Luke CME is bumping

And Chance feels the Holy Ghost cuz how could you not with a musical accompaniment this lit

And I catch the spirit from over 2,000 miles away as Chance preaches with chorus of what can only be described as Black Excellence emanating from the stage

Like my daddy ain't a pastor

Like my momma ain't the first lady

Like I ain't a rapper

Like I ain't grew up on Kirk

Like I don't know the church

The way a choir can fill you with joy

There is nothing like the way a Sunday meal can fill

you with joy

The way gospel can fill you with joy

And I swear Jesus walkin on the radio again

And all the music is free

And I no longer have chains

And it is okay for me to be me

And my body begins to transform into a joyful noise

And this is worship

This is the extension of the hands into the air

This is my soul expressing itself in song

My spirit is the Lord's instrument

And music is all we got

Meaning this milly rock is a prayer

These dances are simply blessings that keep falling

in my lap

As my heart rises to crescendo

And I am overcome with the spirit

And you don't want no problem want no problem with

me

See my being here is a blessing

And God has given me a chance

And He has given me a rapper

And they are in the same body

And it is okay for me to be young

And Black

And problematic

And praise the Lord

And my body is a temple

And my blood is a chorus

And my being is music

And it's all I got

And I will love it

And I will love me

And I will forgive me

And I will thank God for the opportunity to be

For molding me in His image

And for prayer

And I will praise

And I will worship

And I will sing

How great.

Jahman Ariel Hill is a poet, activist, student, and teacher. Currently at the University of Alabama, Jahman is obtaining Master's degrees in both Communication Studies and Women's Studies. He holds a Bachelor's Degree in International Studies with a focus in Middle East Relations. Jahman is a Graduate Teaching Assistant, teaching public speaking and researching protest rhetoric and theory of disruption. His activism with the #WeAreDone organization led to the opening of an Intercultural Diversity Center at the University of Alabama. A member of the BamaSlam Poetry team, Jahman aims to combine his passions of protest, black identity, and foreign policy on the stage through the performance of poetry. He also loves bacon.